Easter Crafts

by Anita Yasuda • illustrated by Mernie Gallagher-Cole

Published by The Child's World®
1980 Lookout Drive • Mankato, MN 56003-1705
800-599-READ • www.childsworld.com

Acknowledgments
The Child's World®: Mary Swensen, Publishing Director
Red Line Editorial: Editorial direction and production
The Design Lab: Design

Photographs ©: iStockphoto, 4

ISBN 9781503808171
LCCN 2015958108

Printed in the United States of America
Mankato, MN
June, 2016
PA02298

About the Author
Anita Yasuda is the author of more than 100 books for children. She enjoys writing biographies, books about science, social studies, and chapter books. Yasuda lives with her family in Huntington Beach, California, where you can find her on most days walking her dog along the shore.

About the Illustrator
Mernie Gallagher-Cole is an artist living in West Chester, Pennsylvania. She has illustrated many books, games, and puzzles for children. She loves crafts and tries to be creative every day.

Table of Contents

Introduction to Easter

People in many countries celebrate Easter in the spring. It is a special holiday for **Christians**. There are many different Easter **customs**. People go to church and pray. They may put on new clothes. They host egg hunts and have fun.

Easter is a time for Christians to honor Jesus. According to the Bible, Jesus lived more than 2,000 years ago. After his death, his body was put in a **tomb**. A few days later his

Children look for candy-filled eggs on Easter Sunday.

followers found it empty. They were filled with joy. Christians believe that Jesus came back to life.

Easter is held on a different Sunday each year. Usually, Easter is held some time between March 22 and April 25. Getting ready for Easter begins six weeks before. This period is called Lent. People often give up something during Lent. They do this to appreciate what they have been given. Children may stop playing video games. Some people give up eating certain foods, such as meat.

The seven days before Easter are called Holy Week. Easter Sunday is the most important day. In the morning, Christians go to church. They celebrate that Jesus has risen from the dead.

Easter can also mean spring. Children hope the Easter bunny will come and bring treats. The White House holds an Easter egg roll race. People dye and paint eggs. They make paper flowers and put on parades. Families and friends get together to celebrate.

Candy-in-Bloom Basket

Easter baskets are an old custom. Long ago, children made nests for the Easter bunny's eggs. Later, they used hats and bonnets. They hoped to wake up to candy. Make a pretty basket for your eggs.

MATERIALS

- ☐ Scissors
- ☐ Wrapping paper
- ☐ Ruler
- ☐ Glue
- ☐ Brown paper lunch bag
- ☐ Clear tape
- ☐ Stapler
- ☐ Ribbon
- ☐ Scrap paper
- ☐ Small buttons

STEPS

1. Using a ruler and a scissors, measure and cut a strip of wrapping paper 2 inches (5.1 cm) by 11 inches (28 cm). This will be the watering can handle. Put a dot of glue on both ends of the strip. Form a letter *D* with the strip. Glue it to a short side of the lunch bag.

2. Cut a rectangle 8.5 inches (22 cm) by 11 inches (28 cm) from the wrapping paper. This will be the spout. Roll it diagonally to make a funnel. Tape the seams. Staple the spout to the other side of the paper bag.

3. Next, make a carrying handle. Cut a piece of ribbon 11 inches (28 cm) long. Set it aside.

4. Use the scissors to poke a small hole near the top of the bag. Repeat on the other side. Thread the ribbon through the holes. Tie a knot on the inside to secure the ribbon.

5. Decorate your bag with paper flowers. For a flower, cut out four heart shapes from paper scraps. Glue the hearts to your bag so the points touch. Glue a button to the center. Repeat this step to make more flowers.

6. Now your bag is ready for treats!

Instead of paper flowers, try making pom-pom flowers. Glue tiny pom-poms on the edge of your bag. Draw green stems for each pom-pom with a marker. Add leaves with green felt or paper. You can also make your own Easter grass. Use leftover scraps of paper. Fill your bag with the grass.

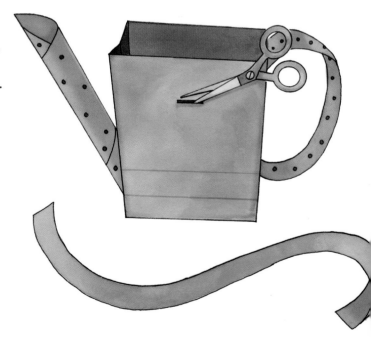

Spring Hat

Some people wear new clothes for Easter. It is a way to be happy about a new year. People once thought that new clothes would bring them good luck. Hats were also part of their outfit. Some were very fancy. They were decorated with ribbons, bows, or flowers. You can turn paper and colorful craft supplies into your Easter hat.

MATERIALS

- [ ] Green paper
- [ ] Scissors
- [ ] Ruler
- [ ] Pencil
- [ ] Ribbons
- [ ] Confetti, beads, buttons, glitter, pom-poms
- [ ] Clear tape

You can use other materials to decorate your hat. Pom-poms make quick and easy bunnies and chicks. Add felt ears and eyes to the pom-poms. Then glue them to the end of pipe cleaners. Twist the pipe cleaners onto your hat. Or make paper Easter eggs. Cut egg shapes from gift wrap. Then tape the eggs to your hat.

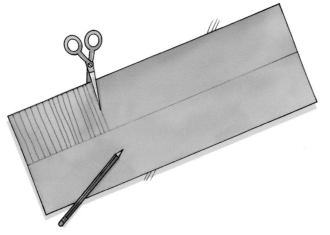

STEPS

1. Take a sheet of green paper. Using scissors, cut a long strip 6 inches (15 cm) wide. Check to see if it fits around your head.

2. Put the paper on a flat surface. Use a ruler to draw a line with pencil along the center of the strip.

3. To make one edge look like grass, cut down to the line. Leave a little space between each snip. You can curl your grass. Roll the strips around a pencil.

4. Glue ribbons and the other decorations like beads and glitter to your hat.

5. Tape the ends of the strip together. Put on your hat and find an Easter party!

Sweet Bunny Bag

The bunny is an important **symbol** of Easter. A story from Germany tells of a special bunny. It could lay eggs. Germans who came to the United States brought this story with them and it is still popular. Make this sweet Easter bunny to give as a gift. It also has a tic-tac-toe game on the inside.

MATERIALS

- ☐ Scissors
- ☐ .25 yards (23 cm) of muslin
- ☐ Ruler
- ☐ Fabric pen
- ☐ Fabric glue
- ☐ Pencil
- ☐ Pink pom-pom
- ☐ Jelly beans
- ☐ Ribbon

STEPS

1. For the bag, use a ruler and a scissors to measure and cut a piece of muslin 14 inches (36 cm) by 5 inches (13 cm) long. Fold the fabric in half so it is a 7-inch (18 cm) by 5-inch (13 cm) rectangle. The edge opposite the fold will be left open.

2. Open the fabric. Draw a tic-tac-toe board on one side with the fabric pen.

3. Put fabric glue along the two outside edges. Fold the fabric again and press. Let the glue dry.

4. To make the bunny's ears, draw a large *V* on the fabric. Put your pencil at the top left corner. Draw a line 2.5 inches (6 cm) down to the center of the bag. Draw another line up to the top right corner.

5. Cut along the line. Leave the bag open at the top.

6. Give your bunny a tail. Glue a pink pom-pom to the back of the bag. Let it dry.

7. Fill the bag partway with jelly beans.

8. Tie the ribbon to the bag under the ears. Your bag is ready to give to someone. Save a few jelly beans to play tic-tac-toe.

Make a face for the bunny. Use felt scraps, sequins, and buttons. Try making a tiny carrot. Fold orange paper into a cone. Add green ribbon to the top. Then tie it to your bunny.

Chick on a Stick

Many animals have their babies in the spring. Newborn lambs and chicks are a sign of spring. This fluffy chick is a fun way to write an Easter greeting.

MATERIALS

- ☑ Cup
- ☐ Sheet of foam
- ☑ Pencil
- ☑ Scissors
- ☑ Glue
- ☑ Yellow felt or yellow craft feathers
- ☐ Brown and pink felt
- ☐ Popsicle sticks
- ☐ Pen

STEPS

1. Place a cup on the sheet of foam. Using a pencil, trace around the base of the cup. Then cut the circle out using scissors.

2. Glue felt or feathers to one side of the foam circle. Let it dry. Repeat on the other side.

3. Cut eyes and a beak from the brown felt. Cut two circles for cheeks from the pink felt. Glue the pieces to one side of the foam circle. Add a feather tail to the other side.

4. Write an Easter message on the Popsicle stick with pen. Maybe something like "Wishing you a Happy Easter!"

5. Use scissors to poke a small hole in the bottom of the foam circle. Add a drop of glue to the stick. Push the stick into the hole. Your chick on a stick is ready to give. Why not make another one?

Lovely Lilies Bouquet

The palm branch is a symbol of Easter. In Roman times, people waved palm branches at royalty. Lilies are another sign of Easter. They bloom in the spring. These white flowers are a sign of joy and light. People decorate with lilies around Easter. Make lilies to give to someone you love.

MATERIALS

☐ Yellow, green, and pink pipe cleaners
☐ Pencils
☐ Mini cupcake liners
☐ Clear tape
☐ Two colors of green craft paper
☐ Ruler
☐ Scissors

STEPS

1. To make a lily, take a yellow pipe cleaner. Wrap 2 inches (5.1 cm) of the pipe cleaner around a pencil. Carefully remove the pipe cleaner and set it aside.

2. Pick up your cupcake liner. Place the yellow pipe cleaner on one edge. The curled part will be in the center. Pinch the bottom of the liner around the pipe cleaner and tape it. Bend the edges of the liner back to form the flower. Repeat steps 1 and 2 as many times as you would like. How many lilies will be in your **bouquet**?

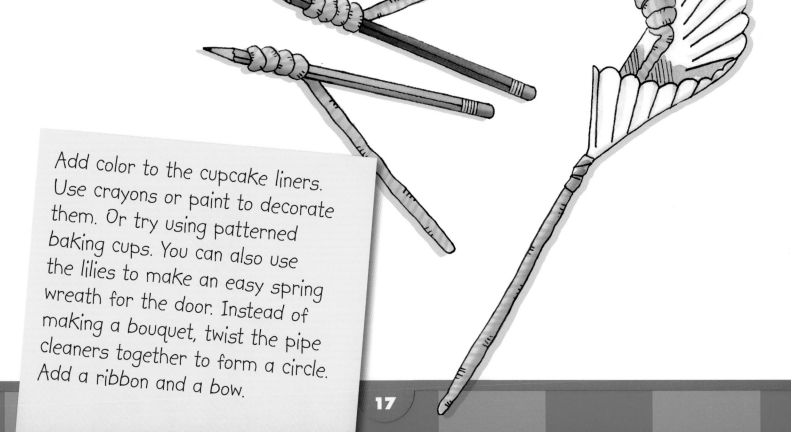

Add color to the cupcake liners. Use crayons or paint to decorate them. Or try using patterned baking cups. You can also use the lilies to make an easy spring wreath for the door. Instead of making a bouquet, twist the pipe cleaners together to form a circle. Add a ribbon and a bow.

3. For a palm leaf, draw a 3-inch (7.6-cm) line on the green paper with a ruler and a pencil. Draw a semi-circle on both sides of the line. Cut the leaf out with scissors. Make one more leaf. Tape the leaves to the top of a green pipe cleaner.

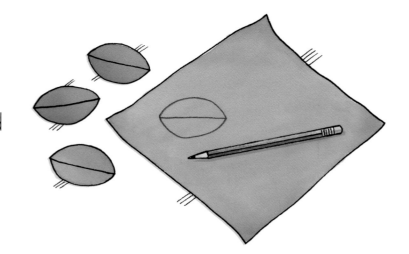

4. Repeat step three to make more palm branches.

5. Gather the yellow and green pipe cleaners. Wrap a pink pipe cleaner around your bundle. Now your bouquet is ready to give.

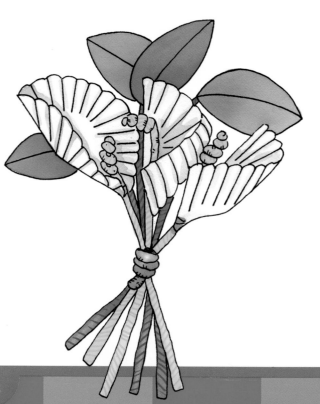

Egg'cellent Garland

Baby birds and many other animals hatch from eggs. This is why the egg is a symbol of life. In ancient spring festivals, people gave eggs as gifts. You can make these pretty paper eggs for your home.

MATERIALS

- [ ] Pencil
- [ ] 10 paint chip cards from a paint store
- [ ] Scissors
- [ ] Hole punch
- [ ] String

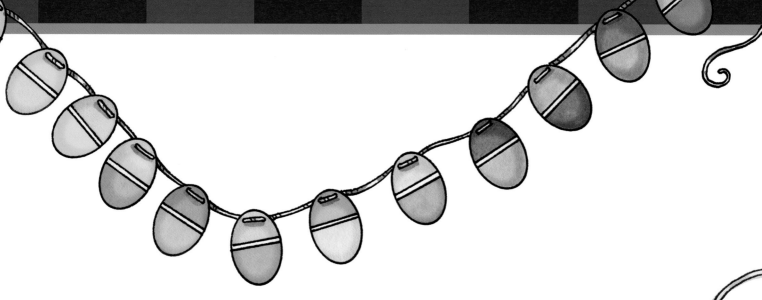

STEPS

1. Using a pencil, draw an egg on a paint chip card. Cut it out with scissors. Now make more eggs using the rest of the paint chip cards.

2. Use the hole punch to make two holes at the top of each egg.

3. Cut a piece of string for the garland. The length will depend on how many eggs you make.

4. Thread the string through each egg's hole.

5. Hang your garland where everyone can enjoy it.

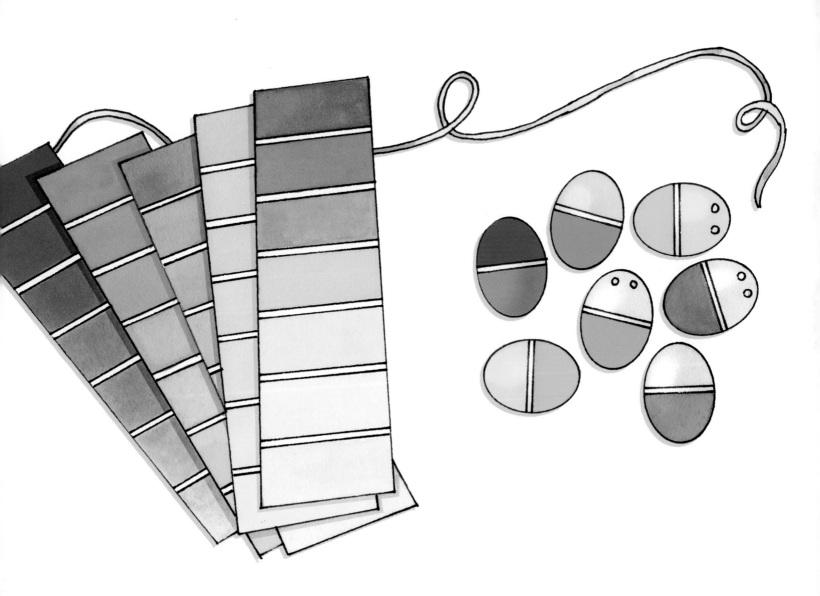

Glossary

bouquet (boh-KAY) A bouquet is a group of flowers tied together. A bouquet of lilies is a nice Easter decoration.

Christians (KRIS-chins) Christians are people who believe in the teachings of Jesus Christ. Easter is a special holiday for Christians.

customs (KUHSS-tuhms) Customs are traditional ways of behaving. People have many Easter customs.

symbol (SIM-buhl) A symbol is used to represent something else. The Easter bunny is one symbol of Easter.

tomb (TOOM) A tomb is a chamber above or below ground where a dead body is kept. Jesus's body was placed in a tomb.

To Learn More

IN THE LIBRARY

Eick, Jean. *Easter Crafts*. Mankato, MN: Child's World, 2011.

Heiligman, Deborah. *Celebrate Easter with Colored Eggs, Flowers, and Prayer*. Washington, DC: National Geographic, 2007.

Smith, Mary-Lou. *Celebrate Easter*. New York: Cavendish Square, 2016.

ON THE WEB

Visit our Web site for links about
Easter Crafts: **childsworld.com/links**

Note to Parents, Teachers, and Librarians:
We routinely verify our Web links to make sure they are safe and active
sites. So encourage your readers to check them out!

Index